MW01674346

Original title:
Born to Create

Editor: Jessica Elisabeth Luik
Author: Luise Luik
ISBN HARDBACK: 978-9916-86-228-5
ISBN PAPERBACK: 978-9916-86-229-2

Footsteps in the Sand of Time

On shores where memories lie still,
Whispers of the sea entwine,
Footsteps echo, soft and shrill,
Marking paths of yours and mine.

Moonlight paints the waves with grace,
Drawing dreams upon the tide,
Silent breaths, an endless chase,
Moments lost, yet still they bide.

Footprints fade, yet leave behind,
Stories etched in grains of gold,
Winds of time, they shift and bind,
Fables of the young and old.

Oceans hum a timeless song,
Echoes of what once has been,
Footsteps in the sand belong,
To the hearts that walk unseen.

Every wave that laps the shore,
Holds a tale of joy and strife,
Footsteps in the sand explore,
Chapters of the voyage called life.

The Architect's Secret

In silence drawn by expert hand,
Structures rise from pure command.
Blueprints draped in dreams to weave,
Fortress walls where hopes conceive.

Arches whisper tales untold,
Timeless curves in marbled fold.
Spirals climb through skies so clear,
Guardians of the atmosphere.

Stone on stone, the secrets brim,
Hidden in each setting's hymn.
Vows of strength and firm decree,
In the heart of geometry.

Rhythms of Ambition

Step by step, the path ascends,
Dreams and efforts, woven friends.
Each beat echoes, firm and bright,
Through the long and silent night.

Pulse of will in every stride,
Stronger with the course of time.
Mountains yield to hearts alive,
Powered by the will to strive.

Destiny waits in shadows near,
Shaped by hands both brave and clear.
Life's grand tempo, fierce and free,
Chanting songs of victory.

Genesis of Wonder

In dawn’s first light a whisper stirs,
Breathing life where silence purrs.
Emerald tendrils kiss the dew,
Nature's canvas, painted new.

Cosmos wrapped in evening's shroud,
Stars exhale from night's dark cloud.
Galaxies in symphonies,
Scribing ancient reveries.

Miracles in fleeting glance,
Fires dance in timeless trance.
Worlds emerge from mystic blunder,
Crafting tales of endless wonder.

Shaping the Ether

In realms where whispers paint the sky,
Invisible threads of dreams unite,
A tapestry where shadows fly,
Crafting worlds in the soft twilight.

Ether flows through hands unseen,
Glimmers of tomorrow's kin,
Shapes emerge, a silent sheen,
Guided by the heart within.

From void, a symphony of light,
Colors born from thought and grace,
Eternal dance of day to night,
Creation's breath in boundless space.

Weavers of the unseen line,
Cradling stars, gentle and fine,
Every pulse a world's design,
Shaping stories in the divine.

In the ether, endless play,
Art conceived in dancer’s sway,
Here forever, dreams shall stay,
Crafted in the light of day.

Vivid Visions

Painted skies in hues so bright,
Dreams unfold in colors bold,
Eyes unveil the hidden light,
Stories in each petal told.

Fields of wonder stretch afar,
Every blossom whispers tales,
Visions vivid, sans a scar,
Mirrored in the moonlit sails.

Phantoms waltz on streams of gold,
Through the canvas of the veil,
In these visions, truths are told,
Timeless, woven, never frail.

In the realms where shadows spark,
Contours shift and dances sway,
Minds embrace the unseen arc,
Guiding hearts in boundless fray.

Explore the vivid, unrestrained,
Where imagination reigns,
In each vision, life ingrained,
Infinity in every frame.

The Creator's Hymn

From silence rises sacred song,
A hymn of life through time prolonged,
Echoes where the stars belong,
The cosmos tuned in voices strong.

Hands of light, the world they mold,
Breathing life in every fold,
Crafting stories, old and bold,
From whispers to the fires cold.

Sacred notes weave through the void,
Harmony in dreams enjoyed,
Creation's dance in forms deployed,
The hymn of love, pure and unalloyed.

Each verse a universe in bloom,
Resonating through the tomb,
In silence, promise to resume,
Eternal in the sacred room.

Lifted high, the creator's voice,
Sings of sorrow, hope, and choice,
In its echoes we rejoice,
Embracing life in every noise.

Spark of Origins

In the dawn of silent birth,
Lies the spark to shape the earth,
Whispers of the cosmos ring,
Through the void, new hope to bring.

Flame ignites the timeless dark,
Stories in each tiny spark,
Origins in stardust carved,
Through the ages, pathways starved.

Growth unfurls in subtle light,
Born from chaos, dawned so bright,
Defying void, defying night,
Life emerges in its flight.

Through the aeons, life persists,
In every breath, a universe,
Origins in sparks consist,
Boundless verse to rehearse.

From the spark, creation soars,
Etched in time, forever more,
Guiding light to distant shores,
Boundless tales yet to explore.

Building the Fantastical

Bricks of dreams we slowly stack,
In the azure skies, no turning back.
Mortar of hopes, we craft our tale,
Creating worlds, beyond the pale.

Blueprints drawn from whispers and song,
Where shadows dance, they all belong.
Foundations laid with whispers light,
A castle forms in endless night.

Windows framed with beams of gold,
A sanctuary for the young and old.
In the corridors, the future waits,
Opening up enchanted gates.

Towers spiral towards the stars,
Earth and heavens bridge their spars.
Magic laces every stone,
In this place, where dreams are grown.

Lights aglow with twilight's gleam,
Awakening the boundless dream.
In this realm we've brought to life,
Fantasy cuts through daily strife.

Essence of Invention

Sparks ignite the twilight hue,
Innovation’s birth is ever true.
From silence springs a symphony,
Crafting endless possibility.

Wheels and cogs, a rhythm pure,
Mechanisms fine, in motion cure.
Mind and metal, intertwined,
Inventive spirit left unlined.

Gears and gadgets come alive,
Brimming thoughts begin to thrive.
Endless paths these minds explore,
To realms unknown, they shall implore.

Threads of ideas, finely spun,
Invention’s weft, projects begun.
Whispers of the past ignite,
The path to future burning bright.

In the workshop, worlds are formed,
Boundless dreams take shape, transformed.
Essence found within our hearts,
Invention breathes; creation starts.

Fables in Fabric

Threads of tales in fabric weave,
Stories spun that hearts believe.
Needle's dance on cloth so fine,
Narratives unwind, design.

Patterns tell of ancient lore,
Mysteries in the weft explore.
Every stitch a secret spun,
In the tapestry, tales begun.

Colors merge in twilight hues,
Legends in the loom ensues.
Tales of heroes, love and plight,
Woven through both day and night.

Softest silks and rugged wool,
Speak of quests both brave and full.
Line by line, the tales unfold,
Fables rich in threads of gold.

Wrapped within these woven dreams,
Life's essence in each seam gleams.
Fabric holds the world entire,
Fables sparked by life's desire.

Imaginative Pulse

In realms unseen, the heart does beat,
Imagination’s pulse, so sweet.
Eyes shut tight, yet visions find,
Limitless within the mind.

Waves of wonder, shores unseen,
Flow within the dreamer’s green.
Night and day, the rhythm flows,
Boundless as the river goes.

Mind's embrace, the timeless flight,
Stars and shadows, meld in light.
Every thought a spark of fire,
Feeding endless heart’s desire.

Dreams expand without restraint,
Colors vivid, painting faint.
Every beat in sync with time,
Imagination’s endless climb.

Creative pulse, forever true,
Crafting worlds both old and new.
In the mind, the boundless sea,
Imagination’s world set free.

Artistry in Our Veins

In every stroke, a tale unfolds,
A canvas bright with dreams retold.
Colors dance in vibrant streams,
We breathe life into silent themes.

Brush in hand, we paint with flair,
Imagination sparks the air.
Each hue a whisper, soft and loud,
Our inner voices, strong and proud.

Patterns form like woven gold,
A masterpiece in hands we hold.
Shapes emerge from shadows cast,
Making moments meant to last.

From dawn to dusk, creativity reigns,
Artistry coursing through our veins.
With every touch, a world begins,
Expression's joy, where love spins.

Visions of the Heart

Deep within, where thoughts reside,
Emotions flow, a tender tide.
Eyes see more than simple view,
They glimpse the soul, they pierce right through.

Love unspoken, yet it gleams,
In twilight's hush, in midnight's dreams.
Whispers soft, like breezes mild,
In hearts of young and hearts of wild.

Every beat a rhythm known,
A language felt, a truth is shown.
Where passion's fire, softly glows,
In secret places, beauty grows.

With eyes closed, the heart reveals,
Dreamlike visions, it's touch heals.
In silence deep, it finds its part,
Unveiling love, from heart to heart.

Crafting the Cosmos

Stardust falls through skies so vast,
In cosmic dance, where dreams are cast.
Galaxies spin in twilight's hand,
Universe waits at our command.

Nebulas burst in colors bright,
Crafting worlds from endless night.
Planets form in silent grace,
Stars align in time and space.

Constellations paint the dark,
A celestial canvas, fade to spark.
Infinite realms where wonders dwell,
Stories of the stars we tell.

From cosmic breath to earthly frame,
Creation sings in heaven's name.
Each twinkle holds a crafted might,
In the cosmos' endless flight.

Hands Like Magic

In hands that craft, a wonder spins,
A magic held beneath the skins.
With tender touch, and skillful art,
Creation flows from soul and heart.

Clay and wood, and fabric soft,
Shape leaps forth where hearts are oft.
Miracles weave through nimble hands,
In simple tools, the magic lands.

Threads of gold in patterns fine,
Make humble cloth, a treasure divine.
Jewels and stones, they spark and gleam,
Hands conjure beauty, like a dream.

With every move, a spell is cast,
In hands where magic echoes vast.
Art and craft in concert blend,
Hands of magic, our hearts mend.

Melody of the Muse

In twilight's soft, embracing grace,
Where whispers weave through time and space,
A melody begins to rise,
As stars reflect in lovers' eyes.

The harp strings hum a tender tune,
While nightingales beneath the moon,
Sing stories of forgotten dreams,
Beside the quiet, flowing streams.

Through shadows long, and morning light,
The muse ignites the darkest night,
With words and notes, they intertwine,
Creating moments so divine.

Each brush of air, each silent beat,
In rhythm, hearts and thoughts do meet,
A symphony both old and new,
With echoes deep and colors true.

From dawn to dusk, from birth to rest,
The muse provides its soft bequest,
An endless gift, a sacred muse,
In music's arms we gently lose.

Echoes of Innovation

In cradles of curiosity,
Where minds explore with audacity,
Innovations begin to bloom,
In laboratories, quiet rooms.

Each spark of thought, each daring leap,
Awakens dreams within our sleep,
Echoes of a future bright,
Guided by invention's light.

Through trials tough and ventures bold,
New narratives begin to unfold,
With hands that shape and minds that strive,
Creating ways for life to thrive.

From ancient lore to high-tech arts,
Creativity rewrites the charts,
Each breakthrough whispers tales of old,
And futures yet to be foretold.

In every pulse, in every breath,
Innovation conquers death,
Immortal thoughts, in fleeting time,
Eternal steps of human climb.

Sentinels of Creation

Beneath the sky of painted hues,
The sentinels stand, steadfast, true,
Guardians of earth and endless dreams,
By rivers deep and mountain streams.

Their roots are anchors in the soil,
Their branches arms that cease their toil,
Embracing all, protecting life,
In time's eternal, silent strife.

The winds that whisper through the leaves,
Share secrets that the forest weaves,
Stories of the ages pass,
Engraved in blades of emerald grass.

Through sun and storm, through night and day,
They stand as guides along the way,
Inspire hearts to guard and grow,
Wherever life's wild breezes blow.

From seeds to giants, shadows tall,
In nature's choir, hear their call,
As sentinels of life they stand,
The timeless keepers of the land.

The Sculptor's Song

With hands like whispers on the clay,
The sculptor gives the night to day,
Each chisel stroke, a note so pure,
Creating forms that shall endure.

From shapeless stone to human frame,
The sculptor's touch, a burning flame,
Brings forth a song in silent stone,
A melody carved deep, alone.

Each curve, each line, a symphony,
Echoes of life's sweet mystery,
In marble veins and granite's heart,
The sculptor's song, a timeless art.

With focused gaze and patient hand,
New visions rise at their command,
In artworks cast from dust and thought,
The sculptor’s essence deftly caught.

Through every flaw and every grace,
Reflections of a human face,
In statues proud and humble too,
The sculptor’s song sings ever true.

Innovators' Lyrical Dance

Whispers of genius in the air,
In minds where thoughts dare.
Unfurling blueprints, drawn with flair,
To possibilities beyond compare.

Inventive spirits, bold and brave,
Rise above the unknown wave.
With each step a dawn to pave,
In the night, they're stars that save.

Formulas scribbled in midnight's fold,
Narrating stories yet untold.
A dance of fate, hearts and bold,
A future sculpted, futures sold.

Trailblazers carve the unmarked ground,
In silence, a cacophony profound.
Where ideas in symphony resound,
A meeting where vision's found.

Imagination dances, unconfined,
Leaving traces in the mind.
In their steps, a world refined,
A legacy of dreams combined.

Conjuring Splendor

Beneath the twilight's tender sheen,
Magic stirs in realms unseen.
Whispers of wonder, glimmering keen,
In the heart of verdant green.

With spellbound hands, the stars we weave,
True to dreams we all believe.
In spells of night, hearts do conceive,
A world where spirits never leave.

Enchantments dance in hallowed light,
Mysteries bloom in silent night.
Through the dark, a guiding sight,
To find our way, our spirits' flight.

In twilight's grasp, we taste the air,
Feel the magic, everywhere.
In this place, beyond compare,
Wondrous dreams our hearts declare.

Infinite splendor, boundless, wide,
Magic beckons, we abide.
Through the night, our hopes reside,
In dreams that never hide.

Spirit of the Artisan

Hands that mold and hearts that feel,
Crafting wonders with hard steel.
In every stroke, a story's seal,
In art, a world they do reveal.

From humble clay to marble grand,
Talent flows at their command.
A touch of magic in the sand,
Springs to life by artisan's hand.

Paintings whisper tales of old,
In each hue, a soul is told.
Crafted silver, hammered gold,
Secrets in the crafts unfold.

Each creation, a love profound,
In artistry, the spirit's found.
From the earth and heavens bound,
In their work, beauty's crowned.

Tradition's heart and modern spark,
Together weave in passion's arc.
In homage to the artist's mark,
Stars align where worlds embark.

Potentia of the Heart

In the heart's deep, a force unwinds,
Binding souls through endless times.
A power universal, defines,
A world of love in silent rhymes.

Strength ignites in tender gleam,
Visions born from every dream.
In the essence, a flowing stream,
Of hopes and whispers, a silent scream.

The potentia in every beat,
Transcends the strife of time's deceit.
Through joy and sorrow, lives complete,
In the heart, our destinies meet.

Bound by love, unyielding might,
Through the darkness comes the light.
In every shadow, there's respite,
A beacon glowing ever bright.

Life's full symphony in play,
Guided by the love we sway.
In the heart, all paths may lay,
Our potentia lights the way.

Builder of Tales

In dreams of golden threads we weave,
A world where fiction comes to breathe,
With ink and heart, the stories bind,
In labyrinths of the writer's mind.

Each page a mirror to the soul,
Where characters take on their role,
The builder crafts with silent might,
New destinies in endless night.

Through tempests wild and tranquil seas,
The pen sails with a gentle breeze,
A castle born from whispered thought,
In realms that tangible are not.

From dawn till dusk, the tales unfold,
In voices lively, bold, and old,
The builder knows each twist and turn,
As myths ignite and legends burn.

Essence of the Forge

Where fires glow and anvils ring,
The hammer's hymn does sharply sing,
In molten streams the metal bleeds,
A craftsman's touch is all it needs.

The forge's breath, a fiery tongue,
An ancient song forever sung,
Through trials harsh the steel is born,
In every strike, a new world sworn.

With patience wrought and sweat bestowed,
The metals shape and stories flow,
In each creation, life imbues,
As strength and art in ruhr fuse.

From rough and raw to tempered fine,
The essence of the forge divine,
A maker's mark on history cast,
In timeless works that ever last.

Cradle of Conception

In silent nights and whispered dawn,
Where dreams with waking merge and yawn,
The cradle rocks with gentle sway,
As new ideas find their way.

In musings deep and fancies wild,
Conception's spirit, free and mild,
Takes form in light, in shade, in air,
A fountainhead of boundless care.

Through realms unseen and vistas bright,
Seeds of wonders take to flight,
In cradle's hold, potential sleeps,
Awaiting hands that vision keeps.

From nurture's heart to birth of thought,
In every spark, creation sought,
The cradle hums its tender tune,
As life's imagination blooms.

In the Maker's Light

Beneath the skies of twilight dreams,
Where hope's soft glow in silence seams,
The maker's light does gently gleam,
In small, unwavering beams.

With hands that guide and eyes that see,
The heart finds strength and subtle glee,
Through every shadow cast and fade,
In maker's light, all fears are stayed.

Each brushstroke born of passion's core,
Unveils a world not seen before,
In colors bright or muted tone,
The maker's light creates alone.

As evening falls and stars alight,
The world remade in purest sight,
In maker's hands, all forms unite,
To dance within the maker's light.

Rhythm in Stone

Within the ages carved by hand,
A timeless song that always stands.
The echoes of the hammer's voice,
Each chisel stroke, a maker's choice.

Granite whispers secrets old,
Of legends, tales, and stories bold.
In every groove and every line,
A rhythm set the stones define.

Silent guardians of fleeting time,
Their surfaces bear art's sublime.
Through wind and rain they stand alone,
A symphony in stoic tone.

By mortal hands the stones are played,
With every mark and each displayed.
And through the years as they erode,
The rhythm in the stones bestowed.

Creation’s Calling

The dawn arises painting skies,
With hues of dreams in morning's rise.
A brush that sweeps o'er canvas wide,
Where nature's artistry resides.

The whispers of a brook unfold,
Convey the tales of times untold.
In every leaf and meadow's bloom,
Creation's call dispels the gloom.

Mountains reach to touch the stars,
A testament to wonders far.
The ocean's roar and gentle breeze,
Invoke the world's eternal pleas.

From clay and stone, from dust and air,
Creation's handcrafts beyond compare.
In every sight and sound we see,
An endless dance of harmony.

Brush of Infinity

In twilight's calm, the stars align,
A canvas vast beyond design.
With cosmic hues and silent grace,
Infinity's brush strokes leave no trace.

Auroras weave their nightly tale,
In shimmering colors that unveil,
The secrets held in distant light,
A dance of wonder through the night.

Galaxies spin in quiet song,
To melody where they belong.
Each twinkle shines a whispered voice,
In universe's silent rejoice.

With every dawn, the night departs,
Yet leaves its mark on dreaming hearts.
Through vast expanse, both near and far,
We chase the brush of ev'ry star.

Pioneers of Beauty

With paint and clay, with steel and stone,
They craft the world, they dream alone.
A vision born of soul and mind,
The beauty in their works enshrined.

Through midnight hours, hands engaged,
Their art remains unbound, uncaged.
Each stroke and chisel finds its place,
A testament to time and space.

From thought to form, they bravely tread,
Where inspirations softly spread.
In every piece, a story told,
Of new frontiers in wonders bold.

Their legacy in light embeds,
In hues of blues and sunset reds.
For they, the ones who dare to see,
Are pioneers of beauty's sea.

Canvas of Possibility

Blank and pure, a canvas wide,
Dreams and visions side by side,
Brush of hope, in colors bright,
Shapes the dawn from deepest night.

Whispers of what might yet be,
Embrace the call of destiny,
Boundless dreams, take form and flight,
In a world born from sheer delight.

Imagination's boundless sea,
Fills the void with ecstasy,
Every stroke, a future cast,
Bearing thoughts that ever last.

Frame by frame, a life anew,
In colors, shades, and every hue,
The future's pulse, it beats in rhyme,
Art transcending space and time.

In this realm where dreams reside,
Hope and faith are magnified,
Canvas stretched to infinity,
Endless realms of possibility.

Chiseling the Future

From rough stone to beauty's form,
Crafting tales beyond the norm,
Each blow precise, each moment grand,
Creating futures by our hand.

In every strike, a vision clear,
Transforming what was once austere,
Passion fuels each confident touch,
Sculpting dreams that mean so much.

From shapeless rock to graceful curve,
In every groove, fate's we preserve,
Our tools, they carve a future bright,
Chiseling stars from endless night.

Patient hands and steady mind,
Reveal the beauty locked inside,
Each fragment falls, a burden cast,
Creating wonders built to last.

The masterpiece, it stands so tall,
A testament to rising call,
In sculpted stone, our dreams we seal,
The power of our will made real.

Wings of Aspiration

On feathers light, ambitions rise,
Soaring high, they touch the skies,
Dreams unbound by earthly chains,
In hearts where hope forever reigns.

With wings that span the widest range,
Flying forth through winds of change,
Every gust and every gale,
A step towards goals that never fail.

In azure peaks and valleys deep,
Aspirations gently sweep,
Paths of light through shadows roam,
Guiding spirits back to home.

Boundless heights and endless quests,
Dreams ignite within our chests,
In every flight—a heart's delight,
Chasing stars through the endless night.

Wings that flutter, wings that soar,
Dreams unveiled forevermore,
In skies of blue, they find their place,
Embodying hope in every grace.

Reflections of Genius

In mirrored depths, the mind explores,
A labyrinth of thoughts it stores,
Genius sparkles, pure and bright,
In the depths of endless night.

Reflected in the crystal clear,
Ideas bloom both far and near,
Every thought, a seed of gold,
In imaginations, bold untold.

Genius whispers timeless lore,
Echoes found in ancient door,
Creativity, a boundless sea,
Reflections bound by destiny.

In stillness, find the muse we seek,
In silence, thoughts begin to speak,
Every insight casts a light,
On the shadows, banishing night.

Mirrored minds of endless dreams,
Bridging worlds with vibrant schemes,
Reflections of a soul's delight,
Genius shines through endless night.

Dreamsmiths

In the forges of our mind, truths ignite,
Visions form, where shadows take flight.
Hammers of thought, on anvils vast,
Shape futures, out of the past.

With dreams as raw, we fashion day,
Welding night, to dawn's early sway.
Metal of hope, molten and bright,
Crafted by dreamsmiths, in starlit light.

Chisels of intention carve pure lore,
To whispered realms, we forever explore.
Journeying-minds, with sparks as our guide,
On the wings of the unseen, we ride.

Invention's breath, a fervent fire,
Weaving wonders, our true desire.
Dreamsmiths, in a realm of unseen hues,
Eternal artisans of the sought and the new.

From heart's anvil, and soul's deep groan,
We mold worlds, of flesh and stone.
In our dreams, the universe unfurls,
Crafting art, from mortal swirls.

Crafting Continuum

From a speck of dust, to galaxies grand,
Crafting continuum, life's in our hand.
Threads of forever, we softly entwine,
In the loom of existence, the stars we align.

Infinity's weave in temporal grace,
Spanning the void, across time and space.
With needle precise, and cosmic thread,
Stitching the vast, where minds are led.

The loom of fate, with endless strands,
Pattern of lives, in tender hands.
An artisan’s touch on the fabric bold,
Crafting tales, both new and old.

Mortals of clay, sculpted by time,
Crafting continuum, with reason and rhyme.
Unweaving night, to dawn’s first gleam,
In a tapestry woven, of hope and dream.

Beneath the heavens, we spin and twine,
Measure the cosmos, with heart and mind.
Crafting continuum, from dawn till even,
Under the gaze of the eternal heaven.

Essence of the Maker

In the silence of creation's deep,
The essence of the maker does sleep.
From thought's forge, to hands so skilled,
Crafting fate, as destiny willed.

Brush of art on canvas wide,
In hues of soul, and shadows abide.
Every stroke, a whisper formed,
In the essence, a spirit warmed.

Maker's breath in clay and stone,
In every sculpt, a world born alone.
Chisels mark, the essence sweet,
Transcending time, where minds meet.

In every craft, the essence pours,
Through wood, through words, forever soars.
The maker's spirit, fierce and wild,
Echoes in creations, undefiled.

The essence binds, the maker's creed,
From heart's desire, to humble need.
In every work, the essence stays,
The maker's spirit, through endless days.

The Artistic Pulse

In every heartbeat, art does flow,
The artistic pulse, with fervent glow.
Brushstrokes dance, with life's own beat,
Creating wonders, we dare to meet.

Canvas alive with energy's grace,
Colors vibrant, a boundless space.
Each pulse a note, a rhythm clear,
Crafting beauty, far and near.

The pulse of art within us all,
A timeless beat, we heed the call.
Through hands that mold, and thoughts refine,
The artistic pulse, in hearts enshrined.

From first light's blush, to twilight's hush,
The artistic pulse, in every rush.
Songs unsung, and tales untold,
Artistic spirit, fierce and bold.

Echoes of creation, in each thrum,
The artistic pulse, forever hums.
In every soul, it finds a place,
The eternal beat, of art’s embrace.

Reverie in Form

In silence, forms take gentle shape,
From dreams that weave through evening's drape.
Imagination's boundless flight,
Gives rise to wonders in the night.

A whisper soft, a breath of air,
Creates a vision, pure and rare.
Within the canvas of the mind,
New worlds awaken, undefined.

With tender hand and thoughtful glance,
We sculpt our dreams in dreamy trance.
Each line and curve, a story tells,
Of hidden realms where magic dwells.

The starry sky, a vast expanse,
Invites our souls to join its dance.
We paint, we mold, with heart and grace,
Reverie in form takes place.

From Thought to Reality

The seeds of thought begin to sprout,
In fertile grounds of dreams, no doubt.
Ideas bloom with vibrant hue,
The sky transformed from gray to blue.

Each notion like a whisper grows,
Into a force that overflows.
From silent musings, loud and clear,
Reality begins to hear.

With every step, a vision gained,
The path of creation now unchained.
From ink to paper, stone to clay,
Thoughts take form and find their way.

The mind and heart in tandem beat,
To craft a world both rich and sweet.
We hold within our hands the key,
From thought to bright reality.

The Artisan's Journey

With chisels sharp and brushes keen,
The artisan, in realms unseen.
Transmutes the raw to splendor bright,
Guided by passion's inner light.

Each stroke and cut, both bold and true,
Reveal the visions born anew.
Through trials faced and challenges met,
A masterpiece begins to set.

The hands may tire, the eyes may strain,
Yet through the toil, joy’s refrain.
For every piece, a part of soul,
Blends with the work to make it whole.

From dawn 'til dusk, in rhythm's flow,
The artisan's journey continues to grow.
With heart’s devotion, mind’s own fire,
Creation soars and spirits aspire.

Genesis of Creation

In the quiet hush before the dawn,
Creation's spark begins to spawn.
A flame ignites from gentle breeze,
And forms from chaos find their ease.

From void and darkness, light emerges,
With steady pulse, the cosmos surges.
A symphony of stars takes flight,
Each note a spark, each chord a light.

With hands that mold, and eyes that see,
The birth of worlds in harmony.
Elements dance, entwine, and weave,
Miracles that we perceive.

Each atom sings in vibrant chorus,
The universe, a grand amorous.
We stand in awe, in pure elation,
Witness to the genesis of creation.

Crafters' Constellation

In the evening's tender glow,
Under stars that softly blink,
Hands of art begin to flow,
As the cosmos starts to think.

Threads entwine in patterns bright,
Shadows dance with light's embrace,
Crafting dreams within the night,
In that silent, sacred space.

Tools like whispers in the dark,
Echo tales of old and new,
Guided by a hidden spark,
Stars align, the visions true.

In the heart of twilight's span,
Ideas knit like threads of gold,
Craftsmen weave what thoughts began,
Stories waiting to be told.

Each creation lends its voice,
To the universe's song,
In this craft, we all rejoice,
Joining where we all belong.

Canvas of Thought

Brushes dipped in hues of mind,
Sweep across the blank expanse,
Every stroke, a thought aligned,
In this world of silent dance.

Colors blend in whispers soft,
Echoes of the painter’s whim,
Each line sketched aloft,
In a dreamscape bright yet dim.

Ideas blossom from the deep,
Shadows cast a vibrant form,
On this canvas, secrets keep,
Emotions surge, both bright and warm.

Silent symphony of hues,
Plays upon the palette bold,
Every shade a word to use,
To tell the tales that need be told.

Scenes emerge and come alive,
In the artist's tender hand,
Within this realm, thoughts survive,
Where the inner worlds expand.

Tapestry of Ideas

Thread by thread, and row by row,
Weave the thoughts of days gone by,
In the fabric, secrets show,
Stories told through stitch and sigh.

Each idea a motif bright,
Patterned in a dance of mind,
Crafted in the quiet night,
In this world where dreams are twined.

Colors borrowed from the heart,
Textures from emotions' realm,
With each piece, a work of art,
Guided by a thoughtful helm.

Tales of wonder, pain, and joy,
Woven in the web we spin,
Precious threads we each employ,
To stitch the magic held within.

In this tapestry we find,
Echoes of what once was true,
Crafted where our thoughts are twined,
Where old ideas are born anew.

Masterpieces Anew

From the ashes of the past,
Rise creations bold and bright,
Masterpieces born to last,
In the dawning of new light.

Brush of time and hand of skill,
Shape the form of what's to be,
In the silence, hearts are still,
Gazing at the artistry.

Every dawn a chance to start,
Craft anew with vision clear,
In each stroke, a work of heart,
Rendered through both hope and fear.

Echoes of what once was prized,
Lend their whispers to the now,
In each masterpiece devised,
Past and future take a bow.

Shining in the gallery,
Treasures crafted from our view,
In this act of memory,
Masterpieces born anew.

Sparks of Innovation

In a mind where thoughts collide,
New worlds begin to form.
With each idea that's magnified,
Creativity's the norm.

A spark ignites the darkest night,
Lighting paths untried.
In the glow, we'll find our might,
Our passions, our guide.

Whispers of potential grand,
In every fleeting thought.
From a pebble, we command,
Battles to be fought.

Patterns emerge from tangled webs,
Of thoughts so intricately spun.
An inspired mind never ebbs,
Its journey just begun.

Tides of change we shall embrace,
With hearts lit aflame.
Innovation sets its pace,
It makes and shapes our name.

The Creator's Touch

With hands that mold and shape the clay,
Bringing life to form.
A masterful dance, night and day,
Through calm and through storm.

Brush strokes on a canvas bare,
Colors burst in bloom.
A vision crafted with deep care,
Dispels the shadows' gloom.

Every note and every chord,
From silence, sounds arise.
The symphony weaves a world adored,
Beneath the endless skies.

Chisel strikes the marble pure,
Emerging beauty shines.
The sculpture stands, a beacon sure,
Inspiring all minds.

Art and craft in each caress,
Of the artisan's tender hand.
The creator's touch, a soul's express,
Across the dreaming land.

Labyrinth of Ideas

Woven paths of thought we tread,
Through corridors unseen.
A maze where every choice we've led,
Reflects what might have been.

Each turning point, a crossroad bold,
Diverging trails abound.
Within these twists, pure gold,
Of inspiration's found.

Fragments of a myriad dreams,
Coalesce in light.
Guided by intuitive beams,
We navigate the night.

Through winding halls, we wander free,
Seeking wisdom's fire.
In this labyrinth, we find the key,
To fuel our heart's desire.

Ideas bloom in every turn,
A garden wild and grand.
In the maze, we come to learn,
By touch of unseen hand.

Palette of Dreams

With colors bold and brush in hand,
We paint our fantasies.
Across wide, uncharted land,
We sail imagination's seas.

Hues of joy and shades of plight,
Blend in our visage.
Each stroke reveals a new twilight,
Of our inner age.

Canvas wide and endless stretch,
Invite our sorrows, bliss.
In every line, our dreams we etch,
A world we cannot miss.

Swirls of hope and streams of fears,
Flow in rivers bright.
Through the palette of our years,
We capture morning light.

So paint, let colors sing aloud,
In every dream, take flight.
Within this vivid, dreamy shroud,
Find meaning in the night.

Mosaic of Visions

In fractured light, dreams intertwine,
A spectrum wide, in colors fine.
Each piece a tale, each shard a song,
In this mosaic, where we belong.

Eyes that see beyond the norm,
Hands that shape in every form.
United, yet distinct and free,
A vision that was meant to be.

Paths converge under one sky,
And stars ignite in a silent cry.
Threads of fate, and destiny,
Weaving stories invisibly.

Together we craft, a whole so grand,
A tapestry wrought by many a hand.
A dance of souls in infinite flight,
Guided by an inner light.

Our hearts, they beat in similar time,
Each verse, each note, each silent rhyme.
In the mosaic, we find our place,
A masterpiece, with endless grace.

The Engineer's Symphony

Blueprints spread like a music sheet,
Every line, a rhythmic feat.
Bolts and gears, a grand ballet,
Precision marks the engineer's way.

Circuits hum with electric life,
Through challenge, strife, and endless strife.
Innovation's silent war,
To push beyond what was before.

In numbers, secrets quietly lie,
Equations span like arcs of the sky.
From chaos, order subtly grows,
A masterpiece the world now knows.

With metal, wire, and fleeting spark,
They sketch a tune from light and dark.
A symphony of measured grace,
In every project, every space.

Through problem's maze, they deftly find,
Solutions clear, of perfect kind.
To build a bridge, or carve the sea,
The engineer's pure legacy.

The Composer's Enigma

Notes that dance in silent air,
Unseen rhythms, pure and rare.
Each key a puzzle, yet to see,
The enigma of a melody.

Harmony that's cloaked in mist,
In every chord, a silent twist.
Beyond the notes, a deeper realm,
Where soul and sound together helm.

Fingers touch the ivory keys,
Unlocking secrets with such ease.
A story told without a word,
In every note that’s ever heard.

Within the silence, songs reside,
Where dreams and reality collide.
The composer shapes what can't be seen,
A waking life within a dream.

With every rhythm, beat, and rest,
A heart's true whispers manifest.
The enigma of their craft is clear,
In every sound we hold so dear.

Innovation's Embrace

In minds that dare to look beyond,
Where ideas form a deeper bond.
There lies the heart of pure advance,
A future sketched by novel chance.

With eyes that see what could yet be,
Boundless realms of possibility.
Each failure but a guide anew,
To paths where only few pursue.

A courage found in fresh unknowns,
Where dreams are seed, innovation sown.
In every leap of daring faith,
A whisper of transformative wraith.

Beyond the edges of today,
Invention charts the unknown way.
With hands that shape and minds that mold,
New stories ready to be told.

Embrace the change, the shift, the tide,
In innovation, we confide.
For in each challenge, we unlock,
A world where wonders never stop.

Lyrics of the Soul

In the quiet of night, the whispers flow,
Like melodies that the heart bestows.
Stars blaze alight above with zeal,
Each note sung, wounds shall heal.

Echoes of past and dreams unfurled,
We find ourselves in a shifted world.
Through every tear and every smile,
We pen our verses, mile by mile.

Rhythms of time and beats of fate,
Guide us onward, never late.
A silent song, both fierce and kind,
Moves through the corridors of the mind.

So let the music of life take hold,
Crafting stories, brave and bold.
The lyrics written by heart's decree,
Sing of love eternally free.

Shape of Dreams

In twilight's glow, dreams take their flight,
Crafted in silence, out of sight.
They weave through shadows, softly gleam,
Formless mists into shape of dreams.

Whispers caught on the wind's embrace,
Visions of futures yet to trace.
Through sleepless nights and starry beams,
Minds conjure up their wildest schemes.

Each dream a spark in the vast unknown,
A seed of hope that’s deftly sown.
Emerging forth on paths unseen,
Leading to realms where souls convene.

In the dawn, they hold their sway,
Guiding us gently on our way.
For in the heart, their power streams,
Molding reality from the shape of dreams.

The Art of Becoming

From moments small, a life unfolds,
Crafted by hands so gently bold.
Through fire and storm, and calm, serene,
We shape ourselves from what has been.

Each step we take, both pain and joy,
A masterpiece, we do employ.
Brushstrokes of choice on canvas bare,
Reveal the colors of our care.

Time molds us slow, yet ever true,
An artist sculpting out the new.
From raw beginnings, we emerge,
In constant state of growth and surge.

For in the end, when we look back,
On roads once taken, and those we lack.
The art of becoming, rich and vast,
A testament of journeys passed.

Fountain of Inspiration

A fountain flows, with endless grace,
Inspiring minds, in every place.
From deep within, it freely pours,
Igniting sparks, unlocking doors.

In every heart, a wellspring hides,
Where dreams and visions there abide.
We drink its waters, pure and clear,
And find our courage, face our fear.

The artist's brush, the writer's pen,
Are guided by this force within.
A symphony of thoughts that rise,
To paint the world in bold surprise.

So seek this fountain, deeply found,
In quiet moments, all around.
For in its endless inspiration,
We find our true emancipation.

The Sculptor's Silence

In marble halls, the echoes fade,
Chisel's touch, a silent aid,
Shapes emerge where shadows play,
Silent whispers, night and day.

Hands that carve the dream so grand,
Feel the pulse of timeless sand,
Stone by stone, the tales unfold,
In the silence, forms take hold.

Eyes that see beyond the veils,
Thoughts adrift like ghostly sails,
Fingers trace the lines of fate,
In silence, they create.

A quiet symphony in stone,
Beauty born where none was shown,
In the stillness, art is wrung,
From silence, sculptures are sung.

The sculptor's world, a tranquil place,
Where silence breathes and finds its grace,
In every curve, in every line,
The silence sculpted, so divine.

Potter's Hands of Hope

Clay upon the wheel does spin,
Like earth and sky, their dance begins,
Hands that mold with tender grace,
Shape the dreams within this space.

From lump to form, the journey starts,
Maker's touch, the beating heart,
Fingers press and spirits soar,
Hope found in each crafted pore.

Mud and water, blended tight,
Transform struggles into light,
In the rhythm of the wheel,
Hope renewed, a common zeal.

Cracks and faults, they tell the tale,
Of hands that never seek to fail,
From broken shards to perfect skin,
A potter’s hope can lives begin.

Each vessel holds a whispered prayer,
Of dreams and love, beyond compare,
In simple clay, a world revived,
By hands of hope, these truths survive.

Melodies of the Visionary

In reverie, the notes do flow,
A symphony for hearts to know,
Visions born in silence deep,
In melodies, our dreams we keep.

Strings that whisper, winds that sing,
Voice the dreams that beauties bring,
Each note a star in nighttime sky,
Where visions dance and spirits fly.

A harmony of ancient lore,
Echoes from the mind's own core,
Crafted by a dreaming hand,
In music, dreams are made to stand.

Eyes closed tight, the world unfurls,
Through melodies, a realm of pearls,
Soundscapes painted with intent,
In visions, time and space are bent.

Crescendos rise, the spirits soar,
In every note, life's essence stored,
The visionary in their song,
Crafts a world where dreams belong.

The Alchemist's Notebook

Pages worn and ink-stained name,
A record of the quest for flame,
Symbols drawn with care and might,
In search of alchemistic light.

Elements in dance entwined,
Seeking truths of ancient mind,
Gold from lead and dreams from sleep,
In notebooks, secrets buried deep.

Eyes alight with fervent fire,
Alchemist, they never tire,
From base to noble, paths untread,
In knowledge, boundaries are spread.

Curved and straight, the lines converge,
Where science and the mystic merge,
Within the tome, the answers lie,
In ink, the quest for truth will fly.

Wisdom's spark ignites the page,
Through eras vast, from age to age,
The alchemist's eternal lore,
In notebooks, ever to explore.

Wonders in Ink

Upon the page, where thoughts do flow,
A world of wonders starts to grow.
In ink, reality does bend,
Where fiction and our dreams befriend.

From quill to parchment stories glide,
Emotions penned, no need to hide.
A legacy in letters cast,
Creating futures from the past.

Each droplet forms a universe,
Through tranquil prose or vibrant verse.
A symphony of silent song,
With every mark, the soul grows strong.

Imagination inked so free,
With tales that span eternity.
A boundless flight in phantom lands,
Wonders shaped by human hands.

Heirs to Inspiration

Beneath the stars, our spirits rise,
To claim the muse, the endless prize.
With art and passion, pure and bright,
We chase the dawn, eclipsing night.

From silence springs the poet's voice,
In rhythm found, we make our choice.
To lift the veil from hidden light,
And share the joy of newfound sight.

Through paint and pen, through song and dance,
We weave our dreams in bold expanse.
A tapestry of human fire,
In every heart, a fierce desire.

Create with hands that touch the sky,
Let none our boundless craft deny.
For we, the heirs of passion's plea,
Unveil what it means to be free.

Architect of Dreams

In sleep's embrace, the mind takes flight,
Crafting realms beyond the night.
An architect of dreams unseen,
In whispered hues of silver sheen.

With every vision, worlds arise,
Constructed under moonlit skies.
A landscape born of thoughts set free,
Outlined in stardust's mystery.

From towering spires to endless seas,
We mold our hopes with phantom keys.
A kingdom cast in twilight's gleam,
Bound only by what we dare to dream.

Awake, yet still, those visions cling,
In daylight's glare, their echoes sing.
Guiding hands that build and strive,
To make those midnight truths alive.

The Enchanter’s Forge

Deep within the cavern's heart,
A place where magic crafts its art.
An enchanter's forge, with flames so bright,
Molding wonders by firelight.

With ancient words and mystic spell,
New worlds within the embers swell.
A whisper breathes life into form,
In this furnace, dreams are born.

From molten dreams, the sparks arise,
In shapes unbound beneath the skies.
An alchemist of fate and chance,
Weaving secrets in a trance.

With every beat of hammer's fall,
Creation answers to the call.
In the forge where realms are cast,
The enchanter shapes the past.

Ephemeral Masterpiece

A stroke of dawn, a fleeting hue,
Colors blend, then bid adieu.
Time's gentle breath sweeps the skies,
Daylight wanes, and beauty flies.

Whispers in the morning mist,
Evanescent moments kissed.
Mortal eyes in wonder gaze,
Capturing what quickly fades.

Tides of time will not delay,
Painting dreams in light's array.
Every glance, a fleeting sight,
Every dusk, a brief delight.

Through the shades of night it flows,
In the dark, the artist knows.
Canvas filled with stars so bright,
Ephemeral in the night.

Expressions of Spirit

Brush in hand, soul in flight,
Colors cast in spectral light.
Heartfelt whispers on the page,
Feelings dance upon the stage.

Canvas bears the silent voice,
In each stroke, a daring choice.
Textures weave a story told,
Of the spirit, pure and bold.

Every hue, a mind's release,
Ventures through the realms of peace.
Depths of blue, a tranquil sea,
Echoes of eternity.

Painter sings in muted tones,
In each line, a thousand poems.
Silent words that flow like streams,
Expressions born from hidden dreams.

Pioneers of Imagination

Boundless worlds within the mind,
Explorers of a different kind.
Charting seas yet unperceived,
In realms where dreams are freely weaved.

Castles rise in thought's embrace,
Invention marks its sacred place.
Heroes quest in fabled lore,
Seeking what was dreamed before.

Voyages through twilight's gleam,
Navigators of the stream.
Wisdom borne on wings of air,
Skyward thoughts, a bold affair.

With each step, new dreams unfold,
Stories crafted, bright and bold.
Pioneers of boundless skies,
Venturing where no thought dies.

The Embryo of Art

In the quiet of the start,
Lies the embryo of art.
Conceived in silent, sacred thought,
Wonder's seed so dearly sought.

From the depths of inner space,
Forms begin a graceful race.
Lines emerge, unbound, set free,
Crowded shapes in mystery.

Glimpses of a future grand,
Touched by the creator's hand.
Images in silent sway,
Make their tentative foray.

Cradled in the heart's esteem,
Ideas blossom in a dream.
From the void, the light imparts,
Life to the nascent arts.

Expressions of the Mind

In shadows soft as twilight gleams,
Whispers echo through the night,
Thoughts unfurl in tangled streams,
Dawning truths to guide our sight.

Meticulous stars ink the dark,
Silent words in cosmic rhyme,
Hearts and minds leave their mark,
On the parchment of our time.

Echoes dance in cryptic prose,
Fragments of a deeper place,
Where the sleeping spirit knows,
Truths it cannot yet embrace.

Crimson dawn ignites the sky,
Canvas hues of fire and gold,
Dreams like phoenixes will fly,
Stories waiting to be told.

Boundless realms of thought collide,
In the sanctum of the soul,
Where the vast and the untried,
Merge to make the spirit whole.

Weaving Dreams into Stories

In the loom of midnight air,
Nocturnal visions take their form,
Threads of stardust, faint but fair,
Spinning tales that keep us warm.

A tapestry of distant shores,
Where whispers morph to vivid hues,
In realms where imagination soars,
Every color tells a truth.

From the shadows, figures rise,
Crafted by a fleeting thought,
In the realm of our own skies,
Stories born from dreams we’ve sought.

Mysteries on the edge of sleep,
Unfurl in endless shifting streams,
Patterns woven sound and deep,
Craft the essence of our dreams.

Silent muse sings lullabies,
To the weaver of night’s seams,
Binding with enchanted ties,
The waking world and dreamer's themes.

The Heart's Draftsmanship

In the quiet barest night,
Heartstrings pluck a tender tune,
Every whisper holds a light,
Casting shadows past the moon.

With a quill of kindred fire,
Sketches drawn of love and woe,
Ink bleeds deep with fond desire,
Maps of where our feelings flow.

Blueprints of the soul's domain,
Intricate in ebb and tide,
Cherished joys and echoed pain,
Etched in crimson deep inside.

Cupid's hand with fervent grace,
Drafts a realm of passion's might,
Love's profound and fragile space,
In the stillness of the night.

Dreams are drafted, hope inscribed,
On the parchment of the heart,
Blending truth and love unbribed,
Into a pure unending art.

Passion's Blueprint

Blueprints etched in fervent fire,
Passion's hand with careful stroke,
Dreams like castles climb up higher,
Structured with the words we spoke.

Every detail, line and curve,
Maps the fervor of our soul,
In its grace and in its nerve,
We become a tale untold.

Clay of ardor, molded fine,
Crafted by a vision clear,
In the heat, both bold and kind,
Forms the life we long to steer.

Architects of dreams we weave,
Building bastions high and true,
From the love that we conceive,
Raising hopes from every hue.

In this draft of passion's quest,
Scrawled in every joy and tear,
We design and we invest,
In a future proud and dear.

Maker's Legacy

In crafted wood and hammered steel,
The echoes of creators feel,
Through gentle touch and vision clear,
Their legacy forever near.

With patient hands they mold and shape,
In every flaw, no room for escape,
Their spirit in each groove and spine,
Remains in form, in grand design.

From morning light to evening's rest,
Their craft is summoned at behest,
A timeless dance, a sacred rite,
Through day and night, pure delight.

In every work, their soul remains,
Beyond the years, beyond the pains,
Their legacy in every piece,
A testament to life's release.

So here we stand, in humble awe,
Of things they built, without a flaw,
Their hands have laid a path for all,
A legacy that heeds the call.

Muse in Motion

In twilight's glow, she dances free,
A muse in motion, wild and bree,
Her steps compose a fleeting rhyme,
Across the sands of endless time.

With every twirl, with every glide,
She paints the air, a whispered tide,
Her grace alights in muted hues,
An artist's dream, a poet's muse.

Her laughter weaves through evening mist,
A symphony that can't be missed,
Her spirit, boundless, pure and true,
In every breath, in every view.

She moves through spaces, realms unseen,
A living portrait, serene, serene,
Her rhythm tells of worlds untold,
Of stories new and legends old.

In every heartbeat, in every tune,
Her essence lingers, bright as moon,
A muse in motion, pure and bright,
A timeless dance in endless night.

Inked Inspirations

In quill's embrace, in ink's descent,
The tales of worlds and dreams are sent,
Upon the parchment, soft and keen,
The whispers of what might have been.

A river flows from thought to hand,
In inked lines that understand,
The quiet hope, the deepest fear,
In every word, a soul is near.

Through nights of stars and dawn's first light,
The scribe works on, with pure delight,
In every stroke, a life revealed,
In every letter, truth concealed.

Pages fill with whispered lore,
Of distant lands and ocean's roar,
Inked inspirations, bold and bright,
Illuminate the darkest night.

So let the ink forever stream,
In wakened thought and midnight dream,
For in these lines, our hearts do find,
A lasting echo, intertwined.

The Artisan's Path

On paths of stone and fields of grain,
The artisan walks through joy and pain,
With every step, a mark is made,
A journey where hopes never fade.

In calloused hands and weary eyes,
The spirit of creation lies,
With every touch, with every trial,
The road they walk stretches a mile.

Through sunlit days and moonlit nights,
They forge their dreams with inner might,
In silence deep, where visions grow,
The artisan's path begins to show.

In every work, a piece of sky,
In every dawn, a reason why,
They chase the dreams, they bear the scars,
And find their solace in the stars.

So let the artisan's path be bright,
With guiding stars and endless light,
For in their journey, pure and vast,
They craft a future from the past.

Poet's Palette

In every hue, a word does lie,
Where colors blend and shadows sigh.
A brushstroke here, a phrasing there,
Crafts a poem light as air.

Each verse a stroke upon the page,
Emotions dance, both free and caged.
Palette rich in shade and tone,
A poet's heart and soul has grown.

With every dip and gentle glide,
Feelings painted, far and wide.
Brightness ebbs, then darkness flows,
A canvas where the spirit knows.

In this palette of the mind,
In every thought, a hue you'll find.
Speak in colors, bold and bright,
Words of day, and dreams of night.

Through the spectrum artistry,
The poet's voice is wild and free.
Tint and shade, word and line,
In the poet's palette, they entwine.

Chiseling Life

With every chip, a tale unfolds,
In marble veins, the heart is bold.
Hammer's strike and chisel’s grace,
Forms emerge, to find their place.

In stone, the moments crystallize,
Ephemeral truths, eternalized.
Through every curve and jagged line,
Life’s essence, now divine.

Each flake that falls, a past erased,
New shapes in granite warmly traced.
An artisan with tender might,
Crafts the soul, set in light.

Strength in every calculated blow,
Revealing depths that few men know.
Life is art, and we the clay,
Molded with each passing day.

From rugged stone to polished gleam,
Sculpting hopes, fulfilling dreams.
In the chiseled contour’s light,
Life is formed, both strong and slight.

Threads of Thought

Woven tight, each thread of mind,
In fabric deep, true thoughts we find.
Patterns dance in endless night,
Crafting dreams of pure delight.

From strand to strand, the notions twist,
A tapestry of what exists.
Warp and weft in perfect flow,
Ideas rise and softly glow.

Intricate the weave of words,
Silent whispers, loud as birds.
Each thread a tale, a hope, a fear,
Stories spun both far and near.

Colorful and intricate,
Every thread a thought to knit.
In the loom of inner sight,
Weaving day and dreaming night.

Interlaced, the mind's own song,
Threads of thought where we belong.
In this fabric, hearts entwine,
Threads of life, softly divine.

Smith of Dreams

In the forge where hopes ignite,
Dreams are crafted in the night.
Molten visions, brightly gleam,
In the smith's anvil, they teem.

Each hammer falls, a spark does fly,
Shaping dreams beneath the sky.
From the fire, forms take flight,
Burnished by the morning light.

Steel and fire, heart and soul,
Within his hands, dreams made whole.
An artisan of night's embrace,
Carving dreams in airy space.

With every strike, the future bends,
In the smith’s hands, the world ascends.
From thought to form, they intertwine,
Dreams of metal, pure, divine.

Through the night, his work persists,
Crafting wishes, forging bliss.
Smith of dreams, with endless care,
Shapes the hopes we all may share.

A Symphony of Aspirations

In the quiet dawn, dreams take flight,
Whispers of hope in the early light.
Through the misty veils of morn,
A symphony of aspirations is born.

Like stars that guide the way,
Inspired hearts begin to sway.
Upon the canvas of the sky,
Imagination soars up high.

Melodies of future paths unknown,
In every heartbeat finely sewn.
Each step a note, each breath a key,
An orchestration, wild and free.

Voices blend in harmony,
With the pulse of destiny.
In the echo of a silent plea,
Truth and vision come to be.

Rise with the dawn, embrace the tune,
Dreams will live and fortunes bloom.
In the rhythm of the soul's creation,
Find a symphony of aspirations.

Crafting Destiny

With hands that shape and minds that dream,
We weave our thread through destiny's seam.
In every choice, in every stride,
A path unfolds, where we abide.

Upon the loom of time we spin,
With purpose clear, the work begins.
A tapestry of days and nights,
In the shadows, in the lights.

Through trials faced and victories won,
Our story's fabric is begun.
With courage bold and vision clear,
We carve a future, year by year.

Each action like a sculptor's touch,
Molding dreams we cherish much.
In the heart of every quest,
An artisan doing their best.

Destiny's forge, both fierce and kind,
Shapes the spirit, hones the mind.
In craft of soul and hands combined,
Our fates and futures are aligned.

Brushstrokes of Imagination

On the canvas white and pure,
Dreams are painted, bold and sure.
Colors blend in endless flow,
A world from thought begins to grow.

With gentle sweep, with fervent flair,
Imagination dances there.
Across the expanse of the mind,
New visions form, intertwined.

Each stroke a whisper, each hue a song,
In the realm where hearts belong.
Imagination's boundless grace,
Brings to life a timeless place.

In every line, in every shade,
Magic and wonder are displayed.
The artist's spirit, wild and free,
Captures life’s sweet mystery.

Through every brush, through every gleam,
We journey far, we dare to dream.
In the landscapes of creation,
Find brushstrokes of imagination.

Heartbeats of Innovation

In the pulse of present time,
We feel the beat of thoughts sublime.
In every breath, a spark anew,
Innovation's heartbeat, strong and true.

With every change, with every turn,
The fires of invention burn.
Ideas rise from deep within,
A revolution to begin.

In the lab of restless minds,
Boundaries blur, new paths we find.
Possibilities take their flight,
In the heart of endless night.

Through trials faced and bridges crossed,
No concept fades, no dream is lost.
In every failure, in every gain,
The essence of progress remains.

Heartbeats of innovation soar,
Guiding us to distant shores.
In the rhythm of creation's core,
Discover worlds unseen before.

Wonders Woven

In threads of fate, a world is spun,
A tapestry beneath the sun,
Stars above and grains of sand,
In cosmic hands, a grand command.

Whispers soft like twilight breeze,
Secrets told by ancient trees,
Oceans deep and mountains high,
Exist within a dreamer's sky.

Nature's brush on canvas wild,
Colors dance, untamed, beguiled,
Clouds of thoughts, a mind's parade,
In twilight's glow, do wonders fade.

Midnight's cloak adorned with stars,
Celestial music from afar,
Galaxies in whispered tone,
In silent awe, we walk alone.

To hearts and minds, these sights are eyes,
Wonders woven 'neath the skies,
Threads of life in gentle tide,
In time's embrace, all truths reside.

Heart Captured Craft

In hands of love, creation blooms,
A crafted heart dispels the glooms,
Whispers soft of clay and wood,
Dreams that rise from where they stood.

Brush in hand and eyes ablaze,
Minds alight in rapture's gaze,
Every stroke a symphony,
A dance with boundless memory.

Silent beauty shapes and forms,
Waves of wonder, tender storms,
Echoes of a thought profound,
In sculptures' grace, the soul is found.

Threads of fabric weave a kiss,
In patterns glowing, gentle bliss,
Needle's path both swift and sure,
A heart's devotion in allure.

In each creation, love is sown,
In heart's deep craft, the truth is known,
Hands declare what speech conceals,
In every piece, the spirit heals.

Elysian Echoes

A realm of peace where dreams reside,
Soft whispers on the wind abide,
Golden fields and azure streams,
A place where hearts can shed their seams.

Elysium, in echoes, calls,
From marble halls to waterfalls,
Voices lost to mortal woes,
Now sing of joy where love still glows.

Petals free in twilight air,
Glide with grace beyond compare,
Gardens lush beneath the stars,
Their beauty heals our deepest scars.

Celestial songs fill velvet night,
With radiant wings, the spirit's flight,
Guided by the silver moon,
In peace we bathe, our souls attune.

Elysian fields of light and dream,
A place where life and magic seem,
To intertwine in endless flow,
Eternal love in echoes know.

Pulse of Innovation

In minds that dare and hearts conceive,
New worlds arise, fresh dreams believe,
A spark ignites, the future's shade,
With visions bold, creations made.

Hands that mold the clay of thought,
With each design, new wonders wrought,
From code to craft, to art's keen edge,
Imagination’s boundless pledge.

Silent whispers burst with light,
In genius halls, the minds unite,
Invisible threads of spirit bare,
Invention's pulse is everywhere.

From ancient roots, new branches spread,
In endless quest, ideas are wed,
Progress woven in each beat,
Where past and future subtly meet.

Rhythms of a novel grace,
In heart and mind the pulse we trace,
Innovation's song, a ceaseless surge,
In every breath, we find our urge.

Foundries of Fantasy

In the heart where dreams alight,
Forge of hopes with endless flight,
Molten thoughts in twilight's bloom,
Cast in shadows, bright as moon.

Within the furnace, stories twist,
Wrought from whispers, love's first tryst,
Iron wills in ember's glow,
Hammered by the winds that blow.

Crafted worlds in secret keep,
Where fantasy and wishes meet,
Molded from the stardust bright,
Boundless visions, pure delight.

In foundries where the dreams are born,
Twilight's forge till break of dawn,
Vivid echoes, bold and clear,
Shape the realm devoid of fear.

Hardened metal of our minds,
Fantasy in truth it finds,
Immortal in the crafts of thought,
A kingdom wrought, yet never fraught.

Nest of Creativity

High atop the branches wide,
Where thoughts unbound and free reside,
Feathered plumes of colored grace,
Nurture gifts in sacred space.

Nestled in a world unseen,
Imagination's vivid sheen,
Woven tales and dreams take flight,
Born from twilight into light.

Threads of wonder, silk and gold,
Weave the tapestry untold,
In this cradle, pure and bright,
Creativity's tender might.

From the nest where spirits rise,
To the realms beyond the skies,
Ideas bloom, unchained, unplanned,
Crafted by a mystic hand.

In this haven, thoughts find rest,
Cradle of the heartfelt quest,
Nest of dreams where hope is grown,
Sanctuary of the unknown.

Dream Weaver's Loom

Upon the loom where dreams are spun,
Threads of starlight, strands of sun,
Crafted with a gentle care,
Weaving visions bright and rare.

Patterns form in the silent night,
Shimmering in the pale moonlight,
Every thread a tale untold,
Woven depths of blue and gold.

Hand and heart in rhythm blend,
Crafting dreams that never end,
Through the dawn and twilight's kiss,
Dreams entwined in perfect bliss.

Whispers guide the weaver's hand,
Mystic tales from distant lands,
Warps and wefts of pure delight,
Spin the fabric through the night.

On the loom of endless stars,
Dreams are spun as rich memoirs,
In each weave a world anew,
Dreams take flight as dreams ensue.

Dreams Painted in Reality

Brush of hope on canvas bright,
Colors born from dark to light,
Dreams take form in hues so bold,
Stories in the strokes unfold.

Palette rich with life’s delight,
Dreams in pigments pure and right,
From the mind's eye to the frame,
Every shade a whispered name.

Reality in strokes refined,
Dreams in vibrant tones aligned,
Canvas echoes silent screams,
Bringing forth our wildest dreams.

Artists paint the soul's designs,
Through the dance of lines and signs,
Life and dream in colors blend,
Art and heart as one transcend.

In these works where dreams reside,
Truth and fantasy collide,
Masterpieces, life’s grand scheme,
Dreams in art, a vivid theme.

Pottery of the Mind

In clay of thought, we shape our dreams,
With hands of hope and a fire's gleams.
The potter's wheel spins 'round we find,
The vessel born in pottery of the mind.

Imaginations mold in creative motions,
Ideas whirl in silent devotions.
Shapes and forms in visions refined,
Life's essence in pottery of the mind.

Glaze of wishes on the surface spread,
Colors of joy and hues unsaid.
The kiln of experience, time combined,
Transforms the clay in pottery of the mind.

In the furnace burns the doubts and fears,
Clearing the path through trial's sears.
A masterpiece, unique, designed,
Emerges from the pottery of the mind.

Each turn and tweak, a journey's part,
Crafted with care from spirit and heart.
Creation's echo, hope aligned,
Lives within the pottery of the mind.

Whispers in Wood

In forests deep, where secrets dwell,
Among the trees, where stories swell.
Gnarled bark and branches entwined,
Lie whispers in wood, to discover and find.

Echoes of ages in rings concealed,
Tales of time and truths revealed.
From sapling to giant, moods aligned,
Breathes the lore of whispers in wood defined.

Carving paths with nature's hand,
Crafting destinies from the land.
Silent songs and rhymes combined,
Sound the notes of whispers in wood confined.

Knotted hearts and souls embraced,
In shadows cast and sunlight traced.
Hollowed spaces, gently sighed,
Hold the echoes of whispers in wood denied.

Timeless speech in silent rhyme,
Leaves of memories through the clime.
Roots entwined with wisdom signed,
Speak forever through whispers in wood refined.

Symphony of Hands

In the dance of dawn and twilight's beam,
Hands create from life's cascading stream.
Each touch a note, harmonious blends,
Compose the grand symphony of hands.

From stone to clay, and thread to seam,
Hands weave tapestries of dream.
In every craft, where skill extends,
Resonates the symphony of hands.

Moments sculpted with care and might,
Chisels carve through day and night.
Heartbeats merge with life's errands,
Conducting the symphony of hands.

In silent prayer or working grind,
Hands bring forth the soul's design.
Every gesture, art commands,
Partakes in the symphony of hands.

United hands, spirits flight,
Together craft a vision bright.
In unity, creation's bands,
Play on in the symphony of hands.

Writer's Forge

Upon the anvil of the page's sheet,
Ideas burn in the forge's heat.
Words are shaped by thought's command,
Born anew in the writer's forge at hand.

Hammers strike with a rhythmic beat,
Forging stories both bitter and sweet.
In iron and ink, bold and grand,
Art takes form in the writer's forge land.

Writers' tools, both quill and pen,
Etch the tales of now and then.
Crafted with an artist's brand,
Flow the sparks from the writer's forge sand.

Narratives stretch on the rack of time,
Tempered with rhythm, rhyme sublime.
Characters etched by life's hand,
Are birthed within the writer's forge's strand.

Blazing truths and embered lies,
Molded by the heart and eyes.
In ink, dreams and realities expand,
Forged within the writer's forge's grand.

Sculpting Dreams

In marble halls where visions rest,
Chisels whisper, dreams manifest.
From stone emerges shape and form,
A tale of passion, hearts reborn.

In every strike, a thought set free,
A world of wonder yet to be.
Crafting futures from the past,
Each sculpture aims to ever last.

The hammer falls, a rhythm true,
Ideas carved, both old and new.
Hands that mold what minds conceive,
In silent stone, we dare believe.

Dust and echoes, fragments shed,
A masterpiece from within bred.
Lines and curves that softly speak,
Of dreams that soar, of all we seek.

A gallery of hopes and fears,
Immortalized through passing years.
Art in stone, a dream's display,
Crafted light from night and day.

Imagination Unleashed

Boundless skies and endless seas,
In dreams, we wander, hearts at ease.
Worlds uncharted, pure and wild,
In imagination, we're beguiled.

Through starry nights and realms untamed,
In every thought, a fire unclaimed.
Stories spun from threads of light,
In darkest depths, our spirits write.

Mountains whisper ancient tales,
Of heroes strong, whose courage prevails.
In fantasy, our spirits rise,
With wings of hope, we touch the skies.

Every tale, a journey vast,
Through time and space, unmarred by past.
In flights of fancy, truth we find,
The essence of our wandering mind.

Imagination's boundless stream,
A place where all things aren't as they seem.
Unleashed, it breaks each earthly chain,
To wander free, from plain to plain.

Heartfelt Creations

In the quiet of a moonlit room,
Crafting love amidst the gloom.
Hands that weave a tender thread,
Of dreams and hopes in softest spread.

Moments captured, hearts unveiled,
In every stitch, a story sailed.
Love's own tapestry, pure and bright,
Woven deep into the night.

With each beat, a pattern drawn,
A melody from dusk to dawn.
In gentle strokes, a soul revealed,
In colors rich and thoughts concealed.

Art that breathes with life and grace,
A mirror of the heart's own space.
Every line with passion filled,
A testament to dreams fulfilled.

Heartfelt creations, pure and true,
Expressions formed from me to you.
In every piece, our spirits bind,
Eternal love, in threads entwined.

Painter's Soul

A canvas waits, pure and bright,
For colors bold, for black and white.
Each brushstroke, a heartbeat's call,
A glimpse within the painter's soul.

Palette laden with life's hues,
In greens of hope and deepest blues.
Sunlit yellows, rage in red,
Emotions on the surface spread.

With every stroke, a story told,
In whispers soft or cries of bold.
In shadows deep, in gleams of light,
Born from within, out to the night.

The world he's seen, the dreams he's known,
In every line, in every tone.
A universe in every sweep,
From twilight's edge to ocean's deep.

Painter's soul, a boundless sea,
Of joy, of pain, and mystery.
In silence speaks, in colors sings,
A heart that soars on vibrant wings.

Printed in the USA
CPSIA information can be obtained
at www.ICGtesting.com
LVHW021134030824
787081LV00015B/29

9 789916 862285